Who am I?
A Book of Riddles

About the Author

Charlotte Sebag-Montefiore started writing professionally for the children's website *Storynory*. She has been writing verse for her friends for years. She also writes lyrics. This is her first book, but Charlotte tells us that there are lots more to come.

Charlotte Sebag-Montefiore

Who am I?
A Book of Riddles

Olympia Publishers
London

www.olympiapublishers.com
OLYMPIA PAPERBACK EDITION

A CIP catalogue record for this title is
available from the British Library.

ISBN: 978-1-84897-744-0

First Published in 2016

Olympia Publishers
60 Cannon Street
London
EC4N 6NP

Printed in Great Britain by CMP (uk) Limited

Dedication

To my dear grandchildren; Lily, Hannah, Flora and Moshe

Acknowledgments

To all those who have supported me in so many ways…

1

I'm known for something girls don't like,
I have a lot of spots.
At birth my colour is all white
and then I get some dots.

These can be brindle, blue or black,
d'you know what brindle is?
You'll have to look it up perhaps,
to help you guess my quiz!

Firemen, and their horses too,
I'm bred to be their friend.
I calm them down if fire breaks out,
a mascot to the end!

I need a lot of exercise,
I do not like the cold.
Often I am really deaf
in youth, not when I'm old!

I slough my hair off twice a year,
which mothers often mind.
Outside, that's great, it's best for me,
inside it's too confined!

Now child, you have listened,
just tell me, what's my name?
If you don't know, don't worry,
I'll tell you all the same!

2

I'm rather humpy, so they say,
I've knobbles on my head.
I arch my back before I dive,
I haven't got a bed!

When I am born, I'm big; I'd say
some thirteen feet or more.
When older I become full grown
and bigger than before.

I swim along down in the sea,
I just come up for air;
I've blowholes, two, to send my spray
ten feet high up somewhere.

I'm rather fond of shrimps and fish,
tasty plankton, too.
The one thing which is certain, child,
I'll never go for you.

I fish alone or with my friends,
I eat two meals a day.
We puff out bubbles, chase the fish,
we swim and gulp away.

Now child, you have listened;
just tell me, what's my name?
If you don't know, don't worry,
I'll tell you all the same!

3

Our eggs are creamy, gorgeous white
with charming little spots,
laid in nests we build with care
in barns near chimney pots.

Some of us have only mums
and do not have a dad.
We're not upset, we do not miss
what we have never had.

When born, we're helpless by ourselves,
can't fly or fill our tum;
a single male may come along,
kill us and take our mum!

When grown, we fly and dart about,
eating on the wing.
In autumn time we line and flock
on phone lines, sit and swing.

For we have very far to fly,
that's why we form a V;
to other hemispheres we go
o'er oceans and the sea.

Now child, you have listened;
just tell me, what's my name?
If you don't know, don't worry,
I'll tell you all the same!

4

Both my parents built my nest,
I am the only one;
fetching mouthfuls of thick mud
can't have been much fun.

At birth I came out grey and white,
by two, I turned to pink.
Why? – it is the shellfish soup
that I drink, I think.

We make fantastic patterns,
red and pink awhirl;
we live in crowds in salty lakes
to dance in and to twirl.

When we've danced and twirled enough,
it's time to have a rest;
then we stand upon one leg
reflecting on what's best!

I have some funny habits,
I'm upside down to eat:
at least my head is in the mud
while I stand on my feet.

Now child, you have listened;
just tell me, what's my name?
If you don't know, don't worry,
I'll tell you all the same

5

A flash of orange, dash of blue
o'er waters still and slow;
fat fish waiting for our beaks,
that's where we like to go.

You'll see me whizz and zoom right by,
we fly quite low and fast:
that's the way to catch the fish
before they know you've passed.

My Mum's beak has a bit of red,
our nest is nice and high.
I'm born completely bald, you know,
the nest will keep me dry.

Those weasels think we're tasty food
which I don't want to be.
We're small and plump, our heads are large,
you'll like the look of me.

We lay more eggs in northern climes,
I don't know why that's so.
Frogs and minnows are our food
we eat to help us grow.

Now child, you have listened;
just tell me, what's my name?
If you don't know, don't worry,
I'll tell you all the same!

6

I am the grandest living bird,
my wings span eight feet wide.
Roman generals wanted me
to be right by their side.

They prize me in the US too,
I represent twelve states.
I soar and swoop in skies above,
I never change my mates.

I may take prey from other birds
with talons curved and strong:
I grip and hold them in my grasp,
they don't survive for long.

My splendid feathers Indians used
in headdresses for show.
My vision is quite wonderful,
I see so far, you know!

We choose to build our heavy nests
high up in solid trees.
We rule the skies, we're royal birds,
we do just as we please.

Now child, you have listened;
just tell me, what's my name?
If you don't know, don't worry
I'll tell you all the same!

7

I'm born in white and shiny eggs
with others, small and sweet;
bigger ones may chew us up,
they think we're good to eat.

You may feel safe upon the shore
or even up a tree;
I run much faster than you think,
no-one's safe with me.

I am not to be trusted,
I'll floor you with my tail;
I'll drag you under water,
it's then too late to wail.

My mouth has sharp and useful teeth,
it opens very wide.
But careful, it may then snap shut
a bit of you inside.

I wear my teeth out eating
my breakfast and my lunch;
I grow another sharper set
to help me munch and crunch!

Now child, you have listened;
just tell me, what's my name?
If you don't know, don't worry,
I'll tell you all the same!

8

It's true that I am rather long
with legs a little short;
I like to dig a lovely hole
which isn't what I'm taught!

My ancestors were German dogs,
a hound I am by birth.
I used to go on badger hunts
in which I'd go to earth.

I also hunted little beasts –
rabbit, weasel, hare;
whatever dashes down a hole
I'll flush you out, beware!

As watchdog, I will bark and bark,
I'll whine if left alone:
so love me, groom me, give me time,
don't leave me on my own!

My droopy ears must be kept dry,
I need a walk each day:
not far, remember I've short legs,
just train me, that's the way!

Now child, you have listened;
just tell me, what's my name?
If you don't know, don't worry,
I'll tell you all the same!

9

I like to run with all my friends,
a sled pack wild and free.
If number one, I'd dominate,
it really should be me!

Alaska can be hot or cold,
I strain against my tether;
I have two coats to help me cope
with harsh and polar weather.

I like to exercise and run
the whole night and the day.
Chained up, I'll try hard to escape,
a yard dog's not my way!

A watch dog isn't really me,
I do not bark, I howl;
I'm curious, and friendly too,
I may or may not yowl!

I have a curvy brushy tail,
Two triangles for ears,
white paws and legs, a face unique,
a loyal dog for years!

Now child, you have listened;
just tell me, what's my name?
If you don't know, don't worry,
I'll tell you all the same!

10

We live in trees in cityscapes
or somewhere on a farm,
we like to eat your seeds and grain,
that's why you do us harm.

Falcons hunt us, also hawks,
our parents watch our nest;
devotedly they keep it safe
and give their very best.

We like to sunbathe, rainbathe too,
we're in Picasso's art;
we are a symbol, sign of peace,
a bird of love apart.

Our feet are right for perching,
our toes face front and back;
we like to fly strong and straight on,
we do not like to tack.

We think we're graceful, faithful birds,
loving all life long;
we change our homes when seasons turn,
we bill and coo for song.

Now child, you have listened;
Just tell me, what's my name?
if you don't know, don't worry,
I'll tell you all the same!

11

I am a clever whatsitcalled,
a cousin near to you,
I'm curious and have no tail,
no more than humans do.

We like to live in groups, you know,
the women babysit;
the young ones try our patience, but
it's rare that they are hit.

I used to ride my mother's back,
I didn't have a cot.
I like savannahs, forest trees,
somewhere nice and hot.

We sign each other if we're taught,
we like to live in trees
and swing about from branch to branch,
with elbows, hands and knees!

I make some things with tools, you know,
and dig fat termites out ;
with sticks and stones or twigs and bones
we crack the nuts about.

Now child, you have listened;
just tell me, what's my name?
If you don't know, don't worry,
I'll tell you all the same!

12

I'm Mexican, that's where I'm from,
my name is now a State;
I may be crossed with Chinese dogs
who walked the Bering Strait!

I like our tiny breed the best;
with other dogs I'll choose
to challenge them and have a fight,
even though I'll lose.

I'm rather fond of little snacks.
I lie out in the sun –
sleeping, snoring like the old,
that's how I get my fun.

My ears are floppy when I'm born,
I tremble in distress:
if frightened, I may have a bite,
I'm liable to mess!

Birds of prey could eat me up,
We are a tiddly size;
I like a toddle now and then,
not too much exercise

Now child, you have listened;
just tell me, what's my name?
If you don't know, don't worry,
I'll tell you all the same!

13

I am a very ancient bird,
an Aussie through and through.
I lived here fifteen million years,
much more than all of you.

My tail is gorgeous like a fan,
and covers up my head;
attracts the girls, I like to think,
it's wonderful when spread.

I clear a space where I can sing
and dance in courtship shows.
My girl will build a fine domed nest
for our chick as it grows!

I'm very faithful when I'm wed,
we're really quite well known.
On Aussie coins and dollar notes
we lend a bit of tone!

Our songs are what we're famous for,
we mimic every noise:
other birds and human sounds,
even girls and boys!

Now child, you have listened;
just tell me, what's my name?
If you don't know, don't worry,
I'll tell you all the same!

14

I am the biggest in the world
at twenty foot or more,
with unique patterns on my coat
that no one's seen before.

The spots go dark when I am old,
I do have such a lot;
I live somewhere with grass to eat
and where it's really hot.

My tongue sticks out a long, long way,
it helps me get my food;
but don't you do it to your mum,
from you it would be rude.

I'm rather odd in many ways,
I hardly sleep at all .
My dainty steps are very long,
my neck is really tall.

So I can see the whole wide world
when I look right around;
what there's to eat within my reach
can be far off the ground.

Now child, you have listened;
just tell me, what's my name?
If you don't know, don't worry,
I'll tell you all the same!

15

When I'm born in summer,
I'm blind and cannot see.
My spines are not apparent,
that doesn't bother me.

I didn't want to hurt my mum
when I was born, like you,
helpless as a little babe.
We're mammals, prickly too!

In winter, when there's nowt to eat,
I have no choice but sleep;
a roly ball in nests of leaves,
a comfy little heap.

My risks are bonfires, cold and cars,
of people, I am shy;
not summer eves with warmth and food,
that isn't why we die.

Beetles, slugs and earthworms ,
snails and earwigs too;
eggs and bees make up my teas,
that isn't so for you.

Now child, you have listened;
just tell me, what's my name?
If you don't know, don't worry,
I'll tell you all the same!

16

I started as a royal pet,
some centuries long ago.
The King, I was his trusted friend;
I loved him too, you know.

He fondled and caressed my ears,
he didn't mind my toes;
I looked at him with dark brown eyes
and black and puggy nose.

My coat is gorgeous silk and gloss;
but tangles in my hair
are for my master, maybe you
to tease, undo, with care.

My toes are sometimes fused at base,
it's in our blood and breed;
I used to go a-hunting, so
when out I have a lead.

A yard or round the block is all
I need for exercise,
I'm quiet and do not bark a lot,
I suit the old and wise.

Now child, you have listened;
just tell me, what's my name?
If you don't know, don't worry,
I'll tell you all the same!

17

The other birds don't like us,
they know what we can do:
they push and surge to drive us off
"Away you go, shoo, shoo!"

My mum is very clever,
her eggs are strong and thick;
they do not break when, plop, they drop
in other nests so quick.

I make sure I hatch the first,
I eat and grow quite big:
then tip the other nestlings out,
I do not care a fig!

I have to build my strength, you see,
I have to fly one day
to Africa; if you must know,
it is a good long way.

Someone always says they're first
to hear my voice this year.
When I sing, the people hum,
they know that spring is here.

Now child, you have listened;
Just tell me, what's my name?
If you don't know, don't worry,
I'll tell you all the same!

18

I am an Aussie but I live
 in other places too.
Traders brought me here in boats
and now I'm here with you.

We're game to hunt 'most anything,
we rather like the dark.
In packs of ten, we're very fierce,
we howl but we do not bark.

We don't get fat, the outback's harsh,
we're skinny, fit and lean;
our heads rotate to help us track,
to see but not be seen!

We pair for life, both parents help
to find and bring us food.
Our mothers try to dominate
and kill the others' brood!

We're not so many, now we face
extinction, dying out;
farmers keep their sheep away
from us when we're about.

Now child, you have listened;
just tell me, what's my name?
If you don't know, don't worry,
I'll tell you all the same!

19

My mother laid a clutch of eggs,
but not to eat or sell.
She left me when I came outside,
I looked so wriggly well.

I'm really very handsome,
I look like one long tail;
and my mouth opens really wide,
I'd nearly eat a whale!

I'm fond of scrumptious mice and frogs,
they're just the size for me,
and when I've had one for my lunch
I don't need more for tea!

I mustn't get too fat, you know,
nor scrawny, weak or thin;
I have to stay the perfect size
my hole to slither in.

I like it there, it's nice and safe,
I rest and have a pause.
At least I know I need not fear
big birds with nasty claws.

Now child, you have listened;
just tell me, what's my name?
If you don't know, don't worry,
I'll tell you all the same!

20

Hounds chase by sight and gaze or smell;
whichever, we run fast.
Some actually use both at once,
we hate to come in last...

For we are racers, trained for this
and working dogs as well;
our talent for our work is such,
that's why we run like hell!

Our toes are shaped for non-slip jumps,
our bodies lean and strong:
we track and flush the quarry out
so fast, our legs so long...

As hounds, we're many different kinds,
for we do different things;
hunting wolves and foxes, deer,
chasing hares in rings!

But I, you'll know me by my tail,
it has a curly lilt;
and when I run, you can be sure
I really go full tilt!

Now child, you have listened;
just tell me, what's my name?
If you don't know, don't worry,
I'll tell you all the same!

21

I have a lovely posture,
I hold my nose up high,
I walk in dunes and deserts,
I look into the sky.

I like to watch the stars up there
without the burning sun.
Sometimes I am made to race,
 I'd rather walk than run .

I live off my terrific hump,
my cousins have got two;
humans haven't even one
and that applies to you!

I need to fill it now and then;
I walk and walk and walk,
listening as I go along
to humans talk and talk.

When I was young, my mother said,
"Stay with the others, dear.
If you stray, you might get lost
and call, but I won't hear."

Now child, you have listened;
just tell me, what's my name?
If you don't know, don't worry,
I'll tell you all the same!

22

I'm not a working dog these days,
I am a ladies' toy;
my curly hair is densely packed,
my twiddly hair of joy.

I used to fetch ducks for my boss,
he was a shooting man;
I tried to take them in my mouth –
that was my hunting plan!

They cut my tail, so it will rise
high up and in the air.
This helps me swim along quite fast,
the hunter sees it's there.

I'm medium-sized or miniature –
that means I'm very small.
Something that is very sure,
I'm never, ever, tall.

I could be black or brown or grey,
Blue, apricot or white.
I like to bark excitedly,
I'm not inclined to bite.

Now child, you have listened;
just tell me, what's my name?
If you don't know, don't worry,
I'll tell you all the same!

23

I come from right down under,
I'm sometimes upside down;
I do prefer the country,
I can live in the town.

When I was a little one,
I lived inside a pocket.
When I grew, I climbed outside;
my mother couldn't lock it!

My hands, they have two thumbs apiece
to hang on really tight;
I need to in the leaves up there,
to keep my balance right.

My feet they have a built-in comb
to make me smart and nice ,
so when I'm comfy up my tree,
I pick out all the lice.

I eat the gum tree's juicy leaves,
I don't have many drinks
If it's cold, I go to sleep –
I have my forty winks!

Now child, you have listened;
just tell me, what's my name?
If you don't know, don't worry,
I'll tell you all the same!

24

I've been around since ancient times;
those were the days of yore.
I walked the earth and really am
a living dinosaur.

I am the heaviest of birds;
it means I cannot fly.
But I can really run quite fast,
when I am forced to try.

Some think my head is in the sand;
I lay it on the ground.
This is so I can't be seen
and so I can't be found.

I'm most afraid of lions,
they're happy hunting me.
I have to kick them very hard,
then I kill them, you see!

I have such gorgeous feathers,
my feet, a pair of toes.
My eyes are quite the biggest;
they suit my beaky nose

Now child, you have listened;
Just tell me, what's my name?
if you don't know, don't worry,
I'll tell you all the same!

25

I came with Romans o'er the Alps,
an ancient dog of war
to fight the Swiss, they're hard to beat:
no taste for others' law.

That was all in ancient times,
now I've a different task;
I look for people in the snow,
give them my whisky flask!

My name is from a mountain pass,
my oily coat is dry.
Travellers get lost up there;
without me, they would die.

As watchdog, I am very good.
My feet are large and nice
with toes and arches very strong –
I don't slip on the ice!

I'm gentle, clever and what's more
I sense a coming threat:
storms, and snowfall, avalanche,
they've never got me yet!

Now child, you have listened;
just tell me, what's my name?
If you don't know, don't worry,
I'll tell you all the same!

26

Some like the cold seas of the north,
some like it further south;
but all of us are wonderful,
our tum comes through our mouth!

I've many arms that stick right out,
I do not sleep in bed.
I'm not like any other fish,
I haven't got a head!

If I have an accident
and lose an arm or two,
I take a while to grow it back
and then I am like new!

I've spines on top, and tiny feet
to wiggle me along;
I open out the mussel shells,
I really am quite strong.

My namesake twinkles in the sky,
my family is big ;
we have two thousand different kinds,
I wonder if you'll twig...

Now child, you have listened;
just tell me, what's my name?
If you don't know, don't worry,
I'll tell you all the same!

27

I am a bird who likes the sea,
though I may live inland;
my feet have toes, four on each foot,
webbed feet walk well on sand.

They help me swim, I'm very good
and never, never worst.
I like flat fish, and eels as well,
I swallow them head first!

My eyes are green, that is quite rare,
I can be three feet long.
With wings outstretched, I fly quite low
with rapid beats and strong.

I like to nest in colonies,
we're thousands in one place;
nesting on the rocky cliffs,
we do need lots of space.

Some fishermen in Asian lands
leash us, it isn't kind;
we have to hunt for them, you see,
not eat the fish we find!

Now child, you have listened;
just tell me, what's my name?
If you don't know, don't worry,
I'll tell you all the same!

28

My teeth are in my stomach –
my goodness, fancy that!
So do be careful, won't you,
or my tum will eat your hat.

I could be white or yellow,
I've cousins who are blue.
But put me in the cooking pot
and I'll turn red for you.

I've legs aplenty, ten of them;
a runner I'll never be.
My claws could pinch you very hard
at the deep end of the sea.

My shell is like a hard tough rind;
inside, I'm soft you know.
I have to take it off, alas,
no room in there to grow.

I change it sometimes when I'm big,
more often when I'm small.
I want to live for fifty years,
I might reach three feet tall.

Now child, you have listened;
just tell me, what's my name?
If you don't know, don't worry,
I'll tell you all the same!

29

We're India's national bird, you know,
I think we like the heat.
At least we mostly can avoid
cold and frozen feet.

Golden, blue or emerald green,
we need our quiet space.
If we're your pets and live with you,
give us a sheltered place.

Our tails trail long upon the ground;
they're heavy, so we rest
in trees where it is safer too.
At night, this is the best...

We eat almost anything –
flowers and cobras too.
We have no teeth, so swallow whole,
which wouldn't do for you!

Our tails are simply wonderful,
we make a gorgeous show;
attract the girls, and scare the boys,
parading to and fro.

Now child, you have listened;
just tell me, what's my name?
If you don't know, don't worry,
I'll tell you all the same!

30

I quietly sit upon your wrist,
though you would wear a glove
to save you from my fearsome claws –
I swoop down from above.

I whoosh and dive from really high,
I fly extremely fast;
my prey's surprised I fly so quick,
my shadow's barely cast.

Our nests are saucer-scrapes of earth
upon the highest ground.
Both our parents keep us warm –
when eggs, they turn us round

When babies, owls may eat us up;
as adults, we're too strong.
We can fly ten thousand miles –
it's far, the way is long!

We're also trained by men to hunt
since ancient times, at least;
we're still in use and popular
in Asia and the East.

Now child, you have listened;
just tell me, what's my name?
If you don't know, don't worry,
I'll tell you all the same!

31

I am a clever African,
my memory's very long.
I like to live within my herd;
I'm beautiful and strong.

I like the leaves on tops of trees,
they're clean and very sweet .
I like fresh grass untrampled on;
I do not care for meat.

My trunk is very special;
it is a sort of nose.
I use it for so many things,
it's like a garden hose.

I shower with it, I eat and swim,
though heavy as a bus.
I roll in mud for suncream,
which you'd enjoy with us.!

We walk along in single file,
we haven't hands to hold.
Our mothers hold us with their tail,
the young led by the old.

Now child, you have listened;
just tell me, what's my name?
If you don't know, don't worry,
I'll tell you all the same!

32

I'm from a clever, friendly breed;
I can be gold or black.
I don't feel pain like other dogs;
I fetch things, bring them back!

I sniff out drugs and arsonists,
I like to help the blind.
I swim quite well, and like it too;
I'm good to human kind.

I like to please, do what I'm told –
I love my master so.
Police like me for this reason as
I'll sit, stay, run or go!

My mouth is gentle and quite soft,
my bark worse than my bite;
I make a lot of noise but for
a guard dog, that's polite!

I'm patient with most other dogs,
with toddlers, children too.
We're popular as pets at home –
good tempered, nice to you!

Now child, you have listened;
just tell me, what's my name?
If you don't know, don't worry,
I'll tell you all the same!

33

We're thought to be aggressive;
bad training makes us foul.
It's really we're protective –
we'll bark and bite and scowl.

We came with Roman armies;
we stayed with German tribes;
we guarded butcher's moneybags;
the burglars felt our vibes.

A quiet little German town
gave us its local name,
launched our splendid breed and kind –
that's how we got our fame.

We used to herd the cattle,
that's why we push and lean;
but put us in obedience training
to do just what you mean!

We love our masters very much;
we're good companions too.
We need to exercise a lot –
to chain us up won't do.

Now child, you have listened;
just tell me, what's my name?
If you don't know, don't worry,
I'll tell you all the same!

34

I'm not a horse like others;
I swim along upright.
I've fins and gills, no tummy though;
each eye its own eyesight!

I tie my tail to seaweed;
I do not swim so well.
I am not nearly strong enough
to hold against the swell.

I change my colour when it suits,
I'm difficult to see.
I can be orange, green or grey;
It's hard to search for me.

My dad, he has the children,
and that is rare, you know.
My mother drops eggs in his pouch –
fifty odd or so!

My dad and mum stay all life long,
together take their chance.
They start each day by twirling round
linked tails, a graceful dance.

Now child, you have listened;
just tell me, what's my name?
If you don't know, don't worry,
I'll tell you all the same!

35

I am a lively hunter,
I never do let go.
I hunt those nasty rodent beasts
and other things, you know.

I hunt with people, men and boys,
where vermin can't be reached.
I seek what's living down those holes.
Oh, hunting can't be teached!

I scrabble down the smallest hole,
not worried what I'll find:
rats, moles or rabbits, I hang on,
my fearsome jaws don't mind.

We come in many different breeds,
we make a lovely pet.
If you don't know us, boys and girls,
you ain't seen nothing yet!

We're friendly, loyal, obedient,
if we know what to do.
We have to have strong leadership
and that is down to you.

Now child, you have listened;
just tell me, what's my name?
If you don't know, don't worry,
I'll tell you all the same!

ANSWERS

1: Dalmatian
2: Humpback Whale
3: Swallow
4: Flamingo
5: Kingfisher
6: Eagle
7: Crocodile
8: Dachshund
9: Husky
10: Dove
11: Chimpanzee
12: Chihuahua
13: Lyrebird
14: Giraffe
15: Hedgehog
16: King Charles Spaniel
17: Cuckoo
18: Dingo
19: Snake
20: Whippet
21: Camel
22: Poodle
23: Koala
24: Ostrich
25: St Bernard
26: Starfish
27: Cormorant
28: Lobster
29: Peacock

30: Falcon
31: Elephant
32: Golden Retriever
33: Rottweiler
34: Sea Horse
35: Scottish Terrier